THE
GHOSTLY TALES
OF
OKLAHOMA CITY

Published by Arcadia Children's Books
A Division of Arcadia Publishing
Charleston, SC
www.arcadiapublishing.com

Spooky America is a trademark of Arcadia Publishing, Inc.

First published 2022

Manufactured in the United States 978-1-4671-9877-6

Library of Congress Control Number: 2022934564

All images used courtesy of Shutterstock.com.

THE GHOSTLY TALES OF

OKLAHOMA CITY

TANYA MCCOY

TABLE OF CONTENTS & MAP KEY

Introduction

Imagine life long ago, a time without cell phones, video games, and electricity. The Union Army has prevailed, bringing the Civil War to an end. Many people are trying to pick up the pieces of their lives and mend the great rift that had separated families and friends. Life was different then. People often worked from sun-up to sun-down just to make ends meet. It wasn't just adults who had to work hard. Kids did, too.

Cities on the East Coast continued to grow. Overpopulation became a big problem. Thousands of immigrants arrived daily at Ellis Island looking for a new home. They wanted a better life. But homes and jobs were hard to find. Then one day, news came from Washington. Anyone wishing for a chance to own their very own land could have it for free. All they had to do was travel thousands of miles away and claim it. Their hope was restored. Men, women, and children of all nationalities from around the world packed their belongings. They started the trip out west to their new home.

There were no roads laid out to guide them. GPS did not exist—there weren't even cars yet. People traveled by horse, train, or wagon. If you chose to travel by horse or wagon, you would need to find a wagon train to join. The place they were about to travel to was called the "Wild West" for a reason: back then, it wasn't safe to travel alone without the protection of a larger group. The trip would be long and tedious. Many people died during the journey. The rest would push onward in hopes of claiming their part of the new promised land. Little did they know that their lives would soon become legend as they raced toward the last frontier, known then as the Indian Territory.

The territory was first formed under the Indian Removal Act of 1830. Along with the increase in demand for land came the forced removal and relocation of indigenous Native Americans. This was the beginning of the Trail of Tears—the process of forcefully moving indigenous people off their native land so that white settlers could claim it.

If you were being forced to leave your home and walk thousands of miles to a place you've never been, wouldn't you cry too? Once the Native American peoples arrived at their new home, they were forced to live as the government told them to, not allowing their old way of life. They were even forced to turn their backs on their own heritage while being forced to speak another language. Years later, they would face removal again as the land they had been relocated to was again taken from them in the name of "progress." It would soon become known as the Oklahoma Land Run.

On April 22, 1889, thousands of people lined up along the starting points of the Indian territory, all hoping to gain their share of the free land. This competition felt like the most important competition in the world to settlers. To win a plot of land, there was a trick. Settlers had to place their stakes first to rightfully claim that track of land. Buggies, horses, buckboards, and even bicycles could be seen for miles, awaiting the noontime hour. That was when a shot gun fire would signal the start of the competition. Excitement was building. Some were unable to contain themselves. They bolted their steeds onward only to be returned back behind the line by Calvary soldiers watching over the contest with eagle eyes. Many people were successful in sneaking in under the cover of night to claim their stakes before the contest began. Talk about a long game of hide and seek! These people would become known as sooners. That's still the nickname for people of Oklahoma City.

With the chiming of a bell and the sound of a gun, the race was on. Each person hoped to claim the best piece of land for him- or herself. Stakes were driven into the ground when people found good land. Some places were even claimed by two or more people. They fought it out in court for weeks or months. Some left empty handed. Some started building their new homes right away. Within a month, buildings and homesteads could be seen, forming what is now Oklahoma City. The race for land was officially over. Many people may have lost their life on the journey to this last frontier, but many more would die trying to hold on to it. With so much death and sadness seeped deep into its red soil, it's no wonder Oklahoma City is so notorious for all its hauntings. With so many people fighting to get here, why would they ever want to leave? Read on to find out about the stories of the many former residents of Oklahoma City that still call it home.

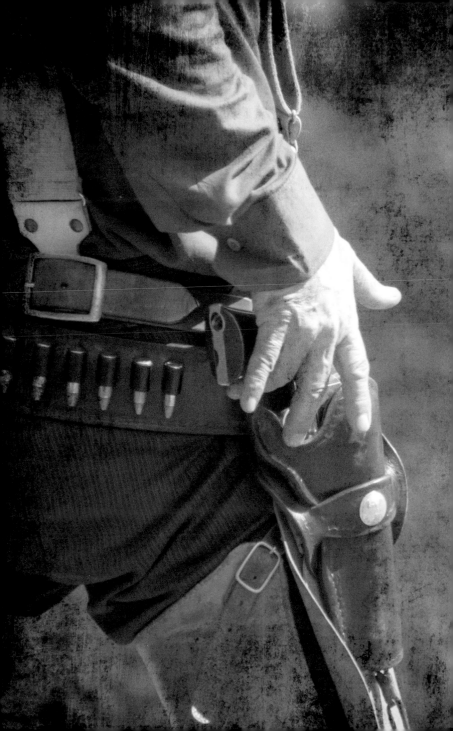

The Good, the Bad, and the Deadly

With the rapid birth of Oklahoma City in the early days, businesses sprang up overnight. Many of its citizens stepped up to help out their neighbors. But, with the good also comes the bad. One such bad man was named Bill. One night, some citizens were gathered to brainstorm the city's future plans. A loud drunk man stumbled up to the group. With his hand steady over the hilt of the revolver strung loosely on his belt, he yelled, "My name is Rip Rowser Bill, and I have come to Oklahoma City to start a graveyard!"

The group decided to end their meeting and meet again another time. Once again, their meeting was brought to a halt when a very drunken Bill showed up. He quickly downed a stiff drink and proclaimed, "I have come to Oklahoma City to start a graveyard!" He continued to torment the town. The citizens decided they needed some order. They soon formed a citizen militia. That's another way of saying they took the law into their own hands. Things started to intensify when one night during his nightly rounds, Bill took out his gun and shot three holes in the top of a tent, once again proclaiming, "I have come to Oklahoma City to start a graveyard!"

Several men ducked for cover while a few of the braver ones jumped at Bill and wrestled the revolver out of his hands. They tied his hands with a tent rope and then tied one around his neck like a leash. The question was what to do with him. There wasn't a jail yet, let alone a sheriff to keep an eye on him. The group of men decided they would put him on a train and ship him off to Texas. What better place to send a lawless cowboy, right? Unfortunately, fate was not on their side. While on their way to the train station, someone stopped them to tell them that the midnight train was delayed. It was not expected in for three more hours. Not wanting to waste any more of their time babysitting the drunken Bill, they decided to leave him tied up to an old cottonwood tree down by the river. They slung the rope over a branch to secure him, making sure there was no slack to prevent him from getting away. Then they started back toward town. Three hours later when they returned to retrieve their prisoner, they found Bill dangling from the tree by his neck, his boots six inches from the ground.

The men set off to find a doctor. But they could only find a veterinarian who pronounced Bill dead as a mule. A group of self-appointed constables examined the rope and concluded that the rope shrank due to the night-time humidity. No one questioned it and no one was put on trial for it. Well, no one except the dead man. A jury was formed and one of the local attorneys stepped up to be the judge. The death was declared an accident by, "shrinkage of his necktie." Three knives were found on Bill's body. He was fined $50.00. Since Bill was dead and could not pay the fine, the court settled for the $3.30 in his pocket. In the end, Bill did exactly what he had set out to do. He founded the first graveyard in Oklahoma City.

The Lady of the House

As the cold wind rustles the leaves, a thunderous clap of lightening luminates the sky. You're standing in front of the spooky Overholser House, which everyone says is haunted. Pulling your coat tightly around you, you quicken your pace. You attempt to turn your eyes away, afraid of what you might see. Just as you start to turn the corner, you can no longer fight the temptation to look. A temptation you wish you could have withstood but it was too late. You stand frozen in place as you lock eyes with the ghostly glow of the lady of the house.

Built in 1903-1904, this once grand house belonged to one of the wealthiest families in Oklahoma City. Today, it sits as a reminder of years gone by, years filled with family, parties, and friends. This cold empty shell now serves as a museum offering visitors a glimpse into what life was like during Oklahoma's early years. Not only does this home contain antiques, but it also continues to house several spirits, spirits who do not wish to move on.

One such spirit is one of the original owners Mr. Overholser himself. A shrewd businessman and a very wealthy man, Henry Overholser soon became one of the founding fathers of Oklahoma City. His home was his pride and joy. Perhaps that is why he continues to walk the long hallways of his majestic home.

There is another male spirit who continues to haunt this mansion. Unlike Mr. "O," this one is not one to be taken lightly. No one knows his name, but many have felt his presence. He is believed to be one of the workers who used to reside in the basement. His job was to keep the boilers running so the house would stay warm on the cold winter nights. The ones who are unfortunate enough to run into him often find themselves feeling the need to run away. If you are brave enough to venture into the basement, be sure to watch your back. He doesn't like unwanted guests in his space, and he will find a way to let you know. With any luck, you might just make it out alive.

Another well-known spirit in the house is the Overholser's one and only daughter, Henry Ione. She was considered a bit of a rebel in her day, never quite doing what a well-brought-up young lady should do. Even in the afterlife, it appears Henry Ione continues to dance to the beat of her own drum. She is often seen in various locations around the home. But it is on the third floor where you will find several items that once belonged to her.

As you climb the steep narrow stairs to the third floor, you enter a large open room surrounded by several smaller rooms. The walls of the room are lined with cabinets, each containing several porcelain dolls. Hundreds of small glass eyes of various colors watch you as you wander around the room. One of the other rooms is the old nursery. Now empty of a child's laughter, all that remains is a few toys, including an old doll house and a rocking horse. It's here that another spirit is said to wander. It's thought that she's one of the family's former nursemaids. She is often seen as a small slender shadow moving around the room as if she continues with her daily routine. Other times she is seen as a full body apparition, usually leaning over the top stair railing, staring down at unsuspecting guests below.

This grand mansion isn't the only building on the property that's haunted. The old carriage house contains a few spirits as well. Various spirits have been witnessed on both

levels of the building. A male and female, both are believed to be past employees of the estate. Not only did they work there, but this would have been their home as well. I'm not sure I'd ever wish to spend eternity where I once worked but perhaps they were happy enough there to never wish to leave.

The spirit witnessed most often in the house is the person who spent most of her life there. Ms. Anna Overholser was considered one of the socialites of Oklahoma City. Her grand dinner parties and galas were often the talk of the town. Guests from all walks of life graced the halls of this great mansion. From movie stars to United States presidents, Anna graciously hosted them all. She spent her life building a home and a legacy of her own within the walls of the Overholser Mansion. She spent a lifetime making sure that everything was perfect in her glorious home. Now it appears she spends her afterlife in the same pursuit.

Ms. "O" likes to make her presence known in various ways. If she doesn't like what you have done or placed in her home, she will find a way to let you know. Once she even opened all the cabinet doors and drawers in the butler's room immediately after someone had left. Many have witnessed her standing at the top of the stairs. Many have even heard the clicking of her heels on the wooden floors walking about the house. Even though she has been witnessed throughout the house, her favorite spot seems to be one of the windows on the upper floor in the turret corner. She is often seen as an outline of a figure glowing in the darkness of the night. She is often staring at the downtown city area. She stares toward her husband's office patiently awaiting his return home. Seeing her is not for the faint of heart.

If you find yourself walking past her home on a dark and stormy night, try not to look up at the upper-floor windows. If you're not careful you might just find yourself staring into the eyes of the lady of the house.

CHAPTER 3

A Deadly Game of Cops and Robbers

In the old days, if you looked out your window you would often see a group of the neighborhood children riding bikes or playing various games with one another. That was, of course, prior to the creation of the internet or video games. Back then, you were lucky if your television had more than three local channels to watch. After the Saturday morning cartoons were over, many children joined their friends outside in the fresh air and sunshine using their imagination to create fun games for all of them to enjoy. It seems far-fetched, I know, but that was how most of us spent our days so many years ago. You never knew what adventure you would experience each week. You might find yourself sailing the seven seas with a group of plundering pirates in search of a buried treasure. Or perhaps you might find yourself aboard a rocket ship headed out into space in hopes of locating alien life among the stars. The possibilities were limitless.

There was one popular game among children that started to become very popular around the early 1900's and lasted through the century: the game of cops and robbers. Many children pinned a small tin star to their chests so they could play the role of sheriff. They strapped a toy gun to their waists as they set out to hunt down the bad guys. Others chose the other side of the law, trying to lead the coppers on a merry chase, never fully understanding what that type of life was really like until it was too late. For many that chose to pursue that type of criminal lifestyle into adulthood, they soon learned that it was more than a game, one they might never come home from.

For centuries, people have often idolized lawless individuals. From Billy the Kid to Al Capone, both children and adults have revered these ruthless killers. In Al Capone's day, the word gangster didn't refer to an angry teenager fighting in the street. Back then, a gangster referred to a well-organized ruthless group of men that even the most powerful branch of the law should fear. These men were nearly untouchable and ruled the area with an iron fist. It was during the Prohibition era that these men started to truly take power. They took advantage of the no-drinking era to propel themselves into power and money by providing what the government had denied to everyone else. Backyard distilleries started to pop up overnight as many people sought to make a quick buck. Many were discovered and destroyed but for those organized enough to plan out their business operation, they would soon turn a major profit and slowly work their way into power. With that a new kind of organized criminal gang took over: the Mafia.

Many Oklahomans don't realize that this state has a long history of Mafia activity especially in Oklahoma City. When it comes to the Mafia, most people think of places like Chicago or Las Vegas. But Oklahoma City has seen its fair share of Mafia involvement. Being located along the historic Route 66, this area has been visited by many and some even chose to stay. Several notorious gangsters have lived in and around the city. One such gangster was none other than Charles Author Floyd, AKA Pretty Boy Floyd. At the age of six, Floyd moved to Atkins, Oklahoma with his family. He was arrested for the first time at age of eighteen after he stole $3.50 from the local post office. After that, he continued down the path of a life

of crime. In Oklahoma, many people referred to him as their modern-day Robin Hood. In July 1934, Pretty Boy Floyd would be named "Public Enemy Number One" by the FBI. He would die shortly after during a gun fight in Ohio, passing away at the tender age of thirty.

Floyd traveled to various locations around the state, but rumor has it there was one particular spot he liked to visit whenever he came to Oklahoma City. Just off Highway 44 on part of the historic Route 66 sits a building dating back to the early years of Oklahoma statehood. Originally this location was not in Oklahoma City at all. It was just far enough away to steady the prying eyes of the law, but close enough for anyone wishing to kick up their heels. This place was an outlaw's paradise. From secret poker rooms to an illegal distillery, there was an array of fun. The local mobsters who owned it had their own system for "keeping the peace" and a well-planned warning system should the cops who were not on their payroll come poking around.

People from all walks of life have come through the doors of the building, but some never left, and they remain there to this day.

One such unlucky soul was Ms. Will Jackson. In 1938, this location was known as the Oak Cliff nightclub. Legend has it that Jackson's husband caught her seeing another man and in a fit of rage he lost his head, taking her life. Many people claim to feel Ms. Jackson's presence and even seen her from time to time. She has been witnessed in the basement, formerly the servants' quarters. Rumor has it that if you sit there long enough you can still hear her ghostly cries piercing the silence.

Ms. Jackson is not the only spirit that still haunts this place. Another more menacing one is seen standing next to the fireplace toward

the back of the building. He likes to make himself known to any newcomer in this location. People report seeing a man wearing a dark suit and a fedora hat. He crosses his arms, and he stares back at you angrily. Then he simply disappears. Many people believe this spirit to the spirit of Russel, an old gangster that used to frequent this establishment. The legend is that he was shot down next to that very fireplace many years ago. Some say it was a jealous lover who caught him flirting with another woman. Others say he was killed was by fellow mobster. Regardless of the killer's identity, the ghost is still angry about it. He likes to take out his rage on the workers around him.

One such unfortunate soul found out just how devious he can be. The bar area is located adjacent to the fireplace area where this ghost lingers. Sometimes he will do something harmless, such as clink glasses together or open drawers. One night he took his antics a little too far as he picked a glass up off the bar top and it shattered on the floor. The bartender working nearby ended up with a gash in her leg so deep that it required stitches. Many employees have continued to witness his looming presence and often try to stay out of his way.

Other spirits in the building aren't quite as intimidating. There's a big burly gentleman standing at the front door with his arms casually crossed in front of him. He appears to be guarding the place, but doesn't usually interact with the guests who come to dine. There are also spirits who haunt the kitchen area and the apartment located next door. With the building's long history and dark past, it's no wonder this location is among the most haunted locations in Oklahoma City.

In 2022, Gabriella's Italian Restaurant, the last business to occupy the location, closed and moved to Edmond. There are discussions of another business taking the site and renovating it into a modern-day speakeasy, bringing back the building's golden years. If this is true, one could only imagine the levels of ghostly activity that will resurface here once again when the ghosts of yesteryear can claim this haunt for their own.

The Ghostly Halls of Mount Saint Mary's

Going to school can be scary enough, but imagine what it might be like to go to school with a ghost. That's what the students at Mount St. Mary's do every day. Located in the Capital Hill district of Oklahoma City, the school occupies a tall historic building casting its dreary shadow on the city below. Built in 1903-1904 as a private girl's school, this dominating structure resembles an old hospital more than a girl's school. The sheer size alone would send shivers down the spine of the bravest of souls. Towering four stories high, this massive structure keeps over a century of secrets in the confines of its walls. During the daylight hours, students walk the halls laughing with friends or texting on their phones. Exactly what you'd expect to see at any other school on any given day. Once the students have gone and the sun begins to set, the building starts to take on a life of its own. As the silence of night creeps throughout the school, a new form of "school spirit" begins to emerge. Those unlucky enough to remain there after dark might meet one of the most infamous ghosts who still wanders the empty rooms and halls of St. Mary's.

During the early years of pre-statehood, many religious organizations sent missionaries to the Indian Territory to help spread the word of the gospel and establish schools and churches. Mount Saint Mary's was one such organization. Established by the Catholic church, Saint Mary's was originally a private school for girls, operated by the nuns of the Sisters of Mercy. It was during this time that our first story comes to life. Or should I say death? There are several theories about the identity of the spirit who is said to wander these halls. One is that a nun died tragically and was cursed to wander the halls, never finding peace. But others say that that nun, actually died of old age many years later.

There's another story about her passing. Before there were funeral homes, bodies were kept in the home for several days to be prepared for burial. Services and memorials were held there for family and friends to come and say their goodbyes. Now mind you, this was before modern day air conditioning. So if someone passed during the summer, the smell would be quite strong. Air freshener had not been developed yet, so only the smell of fresh cut flowers could be used to mask the smell of decaying flesh. Because the school was the nun's home, her body would have been prepared and stored there until the time of her burial. Perhaps that is why her spirit continues to linger there.

Through the years, many

students have reported seeing the ghostly nun wandering the halls. She is often seen walking the corridors and rooms on the fourth floor. Once the school's dormitory, the fourth floor is now shuttered. The rooms that once housed schoolgirls and nuns now function as storage places. There are those who have never seen the ghostly specter but have reported different kinds of encounters with her. Many have reported feeling her icy cold hand on their shoulders or arms. Others have reported hearing the ghostly sounds of her fingernails tapping impatiently, their eerie sound echoing throughout the halls.

She is not the only spirit reported to reside in the school. There are stories about a young girl riding her tricycle around in a circle in the middle of the auditorium stage. Once she is spotted, she often disappears in the blink of an eye. When observers try to touch her, she disappears before they get close enough. No one knows who the little girl is or why she still haunts the historic halls of Mount Saint Mary's. The students may not be able to agree on the reason the nun chooses to say around, but

there's one thing they can agree on. A ghostly nun is one of the scariest kinds of ghosts. Perhaps one day, the ghosts that haunt the halls of the school will find peace and decide to move on. Until then, Mount Saint Mary's will have to continue with a lot of school spirit.

A Haunted Hotel Where the Dead Never Sleep

How often have you stayed overnight in a hotel while on a long trip? Have you ever felt uncomfortable in the unfamiliar room? Or were you excited to be out exploring new locations and sites? What if the hotel you were staying in just happened to be haunted? What would you do? Would you stay there or grab your bags and run screaming into the night? If you'd be scared, don't worry. You wouldn't be alone. Even some of the biggest of men would be scared in a place like that. That's just what happened at the historic Skirvin Hotel when a few NBA players were visiting from out of town.

The Skirvin Hotel is located in the heart of downtown Oklahoma City. Built over century ago, this fourteen-floor hotel has played host to wide variety of guests, including several

celebrities, US presidents, movie and T.V. personalities, and famous athletes. But some of the most famous celebrities that stay there aren't among the living. And unlike us, the never sleep.

Built in 1911 by William B. Skirvin, this building has seen some of life's happiest times and some of its most devastating. Skirvin was a shrewd businessman who made his vast fortune in the oil industry. With some of the profits, he built what would become his legacy, the Skirvin Hotel. The hotel hosted various events including, conventions, and fancy dinners. The hotel had its fair share of illegal activities as well. During Prohibition, there were parties with alcohol, even though it was against the law. They was even illegal gambling here from time to time. One police raid produced a large roulette table. The police claimed it was the biggest ever seized during a raid. The wires and magnets inside it revealed that it was used to help the operators cheat at the game.

Skirvin was never found guilty of any crime. It seemed he was untouchable by the law. He was often seen in the hotel lobby, nodding to staff to indicate who would be given special treatment and who would be told there was no vacancy. The Roaring Twenties kept the parties rolling and the alcohol flowing. No one could foresee that it would all come to an end in the 1930s. The Depression hit Oklahoma hard. Then there were the years of the Dust Bowl, when many people lost their fortunes and even their lives. Still, the hotel's doors remained open. In 1944, after many years of hardship and a crippling car accident, William Skirvin passed away shortly before his eighty-fourth birthday.

Over the years, the hotel passed through numerous hands until it finally closed its doors in 1988. The hotel would remain empty for several more decades. The once-grand hotel that hosted some of nation's elite now played host to drifters. In 2005, the dusty, drab hallways took on a breath of new life as renovations began to reopen this historical site. It didn't take long for the spirits of the past to make themselves known. The first one was none other than Mr. Skirvin himself. It was during the renovation that he first announced his presence. What better way to show himself than where he spent so much of his time—in his chair in the lobby of his beloved hotel. Stories of Mr. Skirvin's return were shared by many crew workers during the hotel's renovation. What they witnessed could not be explained. The building's electricity had been shut off. The building was cold, dark, and dead, except for one single light above the chair in the lobby. The light would not go off. It continued to glow bright, acknowledging his lasting presence in the hotel he loved so dear.

His is not the only spirit to walk the long and winding halls of this old hotel. One worker reported getting onto the elevator by herself only to hear the ghostly laugh of a man. She turned in shock to see him standing next to her. Male spirits aren't the only ones haunting the hotel. A woman dressed in a red evening gown has been seen around the building, walking the halls as if she were on her way to a fancy gala. Often a baby can be heard crying throughout the hotel, even on floors where no children are present. A young boy is rumored to haunt the basement. He was first seen on the day the hotel reopened for business. On the top floor, big band music can be heard drifting through the hallway, played by unseen hands. It's on and near this top floor that the hotel's most infamous spirit resides.

Legend has it that Mr. Skirvin was seeing one of the maids who worked at the hotel. Her name was Effie. The story goes that she was expecting a child and had planned to leave her job. When Mr. Skirvin found out, he locked her in one of his private rooms upstairs, refusing to let her go. She attempted to sneak out a window and climb down to an empty unlocked room. But she fell to her death. It is said she now walks the halls of the tenth floor where she was previously kept prisoner until her untimely death.

Many people have reported seeing Effie and several have reported falling victim to her flirtatious ways. The most famous of these came from Eddy Curry, a famous basketball player from the New York Knicks. In 2010, he claimed that while staying at the Skirvin the night before his team's big game against the OKC Thunder, he couldn't sleep because of all the paranormal activity in his room! Players from other teams have shared their ghostly experiences at the hotel, too. Some refuse to ever stay there again.

Whenever visiting NBA teams come to play the Thunder, they are invited to stay on the 10th floor. Perhaps it's the hotel's way of ensuring a win for the Thunder. If the visiting team can't get any sleep, the hometown heroes will have an advantage!

That leaves us all wondering. Are all the reports of Effie true encounters or just a form of psychological warfare to weaken the opponent's ability to play? No evidence has even been found to prove Effie's story is true. But then again, not all history is written down.

Often, it's told over a campfire or spoken about around the kitchen table turning the bits of true history into legends and folklore.

Should you get lucky enough to visit the Skirvin, you might want to keep your eyes and ears open. You never know who you might run into while walking along the empty halls of this hotel. But if you do run into Effie, tell her thank you. The Thunder need all the help they can get!

A Witch in the Kitchen

Across the United States, there are many places where you can find what's called a "cry baby" bridge. That's a place where people say a baby's cry can be heard when there's no child in sight. Oklahoma is said to have at least three of these bridges. One of them is in the southeast side of Oklahoma City near a small lake known as Kitchen Lake.

This area is steeped in folklore and legends. Many who wish to get a glimpse into the paranormal world travel here in hopes of seeing something strange. Some come here to party with friends or see if they can scare each other with ghostly tales like the one about how the bridge came to be known as a cry baby bridge.

Legend has it that a mother was driving along the old road with her newborn baby during a heavy rainstorm. The rain had caused the river to swell. She tried to cross the rickety bride, but it gave way, and the car was swallowed in the rolling waves. Both mother and child perished. Several days later,

a policeman noticed the wrecked car and went to investigate. When he looked through the car window, he saw the mother and child laying lifeless inside.

Stories soon began to spread about the incident. Not long after, people started to report hearing a baby's cry piercing through the night air close to the bridge. It is even said that if you park your car in that area for too long, the battery in the car will die.

The mother and child are not the only spirits rumored to haunt this area. There is another tale much more sinister lurking along the shorelines of Kitchen Lake. Depending on who might be telling the story, this spirit involves a witch who lived in an old home in that same area. Some people even claim that the mother and child were on their way to see her the night they died.

Some people believe the old woman who lived by the lake was not a witch. They think

 she might have just been a traditional healer who blended herbs and other natural healing agents to help the sick. But some insist she was an old crone who would lurk in the trees waiting to exact revenge on those who had done her wrong.

She was said to practice black magic which caused a strange glowing smoke to rise from the chimney of her cabin. One version of the folklore states that while she was conjuring one night, her evil fire got out of control, consuming her home and her life along with it. In another version of the story, neighbors were fearful of her power, and locked her up in her own home, then set it ablaze. One thing is consistent in the stories: an older woman died in the house when it caught fire, leaving only the foundation and chimney standing. Over the years, this location has become a popular spot for teenagers and young adults wishing to have some spooky fun. The chimney that once stood here has been long since demolished by a group of rowdy partiers leaving the stories and history of the location scattered across the grounds. Some claim they can still see the eerie smoke rising from the old chimney.

According to legend, if you leave anything inside the boundaries of the old foundation, it will light and smolder as if being set ablaze by an unseen hand. With each passing year, the story changes and more stories of ghostly

apparitions emerge. Many more deaths have occurred both natural and unnatural in and around the lake, leaving yet another story to be told of the ghostly tales of Kitchen Lake.

Behold the Mighty Thunderbird

In the tradition of most Native American tribes who live in Oklahoma, the thunderbird is a mystical creature said to live on mountain tops above the clouds. This mighty bird watches over humans, protecting them. But at times it is also known to punish those who do wrong. With the flapping of its mighty wings, a large crash of thunder can be heard. That's what gives this majestic mythical creature its name.

This legend is so common in the history of Oklahoma and the Indian Territory, that it was chosen as the mascot for the region's newly formed military division, the 45th Infantry. Assembled in 1923, soldiers from four states joined together to form this division, which became known as one of the best divisions in the US military. These men and women were so tough, it appears even death couldn't keep them down. In their honor, a museum was dedicated, showcasing some of their achievements as well as highlighting past military conflicts dating back to the Civil War. The building that houses the museum now didn't start as a museum. Originally it was an officer's club, where the military commanders would come to enjoy a night of music and dancing. It appears a few of those spirits may still be kicking up their heels in this location when the lights go down.

Military vehicles line the museum grounds, from large army tanks to helicopters. You can almost picture the soldiers manning the guns ready to take flight at any given moment. If you listen closely, you might even be able to hear the drumming of footsteps beating a timely rhythm as the boots of soldiers thump loudly on the grounds. The whipping of the flags in the Oklahoma wind mingles with the clinking of the ropes on the flagpole, sending an eerie cry into the night. Across the road lie the remains of dedicated soldiers who gave their lives to help preserve our freedom.

Inside the museum, there are a number of different kinds of military artifacts. Guns from several different eras and locations can be seen here, as well as uniforms, military equipment, medical supplies, and even an ambulance or two. Some of the most interesting items belong to Hitler himself, obtained while invading his personal bunker. Other items were obtained when some of the 45th soldiers liberated one of the Nazi concentration camps. With all of these items and history, it's no wonder the building is practically overflowing with ghostly activity.

Paranormal investigators have reported a multitude of ghostly experiences in and around the museum. Some of the spirits seem to reside near one of the old ambulances in the large motor pool area. Reports of ghostly whispers can often be heard there. Some report experiencing the touch of an icy cold hand reaching out to anyone who is brave enough to walk by. The mannequins around the room are dressed in the uniforms of soldiers from the past. Their eyes appear to follow you around the room. Footsteps can be heard walking among the military vehicles stored within these walls, often causing a guest to yell out, "is anyone there?" Their questions are met by the dead still silence of the room. The motor pool area is not the only room to contain a ghostly presence.

Another area where ghostly activity has been witnessed is the old chapel in the back of the museum. It was built to offer any visitor a chance to pray or grieve for any loved ones who may have perished during one of the wars. Some say the ghostly spirit who has been seen

here is one of the very men who had built the chapel many years before. His spirit is often felt sitting among the pews, as if ready to offer any comfort to those in need. Several psychics who have visited this area has reported seeing and feeling his presence. It is said to bring a sense of peace, not of fright.

The same can't be said about some of the other spirits that linger farther back into the dark corridors of the museum. One such apparition is found in the Civil War area. Here, people say they feel an overwhelming sense of doom as fear and anxiety take over their souls. Perhaps it's not even a spirit that's causing this disruption, but rather the intense emotions that soldiers felt during such a dark time in American history.

From the phantom sound of marching soldiers to the cold chilled touch from a ghostly hand, you never know what you might experience at this haunted military museum. One thing is for certain, history abounds with the walls of the 45th Infantry Museum.

A Boot Scoot'n Boo-gy

Have you ever heard a spirit call out your name? How do you think it might make you feel if you did? Imagine yourself alone in a room preparing for a night of investigations in an old historic location while your friends are working downstairs. As you're setting up the cameras for the long night ahead, you hear a male voice call your name from the bottom of the stairs. You quickly walk over and yell back down to find out who was calling you. No one answers. You call out again. Still no answer. You descend the small flight of stairs only to find no one waiting there. You then walk across a large wooden dance floor to where the rest of your teammates are. You ask who needed you. As they look back and forth to one another, each one denies ever calling out or even being near the stairs at all. There's only one male in the building with you that night. He denies having called you. You suddenly realize that you just witnessed your first paranormal activity of the night. It appears that the ghost knows you by name. Would you be scared then? It

can be a little unsettling. I should know since that is exactly what happened to me one night. Little did I know it would not be the last time something strange happened to me in this spooky location.

On the outskirts of Oklahoma City, there's an old bar. The building was constructed a little over seventy years ago. It was once a very popular location for country music enthusiasts. It played host to some of the country's biggest country music stars. It's rumored that Elvis even played a time or two. Folks would come from all over to listen to some of the most popular singers of the time and to take a few spins around the dance floor. With the passing of time, the Oklahoma City started moving more northward than south. The crowds slowly started to drift away, and the once booming club called the Sooner Corral began to fall into disrepair. The money to fix it wasn't easy to come by. The building changed hands a few times over the years. But one thing always stayed the same. The ghosts chose to never leave.

One such spirit goes by the name of Taz. He's often seen around and behind the bar. Staff say that he likes the bar to be kept nice and tidy. If something is left out of place or not cleaned to his approval, he tends to throw a tantrum. Glasses and bottles will be tossed around. A coaster will take flight as if being tossed by unseen hands. Sometimes Taz likes to make his presence known by walking around the bar area, clinking his spurs against the old wooden floors. Those unlucky enough to run into him describe him as a rough-looking sort

sporting a wide brim hat and a long brown trench coat. To help keep the peace, the staff started leaving him a drink each night, hoping to appease the cranky spirit who believed he ran the place.

Another bossy spirit often seen in the club is one the staff members liked to call Griz. A large man often seen with his arms crossed on his chest, he is believed to have been a past employee of the night club. Perhaps he was a bouncer once hired to keep the peace. It appears Griz never let anything keep him from doing his job. Not even death. He's not someone you would care to run into, as one former employee found out. He had been cleaning one of the restrooms when he noticed a large man

standing in the doorway blocking the way out. The man stood with his eyes staring daggers into the employee, his large arms crossed tightly against his chest. The employee tried to scoot around him, but with little room to maneuver, he ended up bumping him in the shoulder as he quickly tried to walk past. As he turned to see if the man had followed, all he could see was an empty space where he once stood. He had simply disappeared into thin air.

It's not only men who haunt this location. Ghostly women have been seen around building, especially in the old office area upstairs. This is the very office where I was standing when the male spirit called out my name. The room is small with an open sitting area and a bathroom. It appears to be like any other room, but this room holds many secrets within its walls. One such secret was in a small alcove area by the north wall. There you will see a small bookcase—about three to four feet high—built into the wall. No books can be found there, only a few knickknacks covered in dust. This bookcase is no ordinary bookcase. If you know its history, then you might know that if you pull on one of the shelves, the bookcase will give way. You see, the bookcase is actually a hidden room. There have been many rumors and legends attached to this secret room over the years, but no real documents have ever revealed the room's purpose. One can only imagine what might have occurred over the years.

The spirits of the old Sooner Corral lived on over the years always making their presence know to staff and patrons. Whether it was the clinking of spurs or a chair that went scooting across the floor on its own, this building remained active with ghostly activity. Unfortunately, in 2021, a large fire broke out, causing extensive damage and leaving the building and its history

smoking in a pile of embers. Perhaps the ghosts are now free to wander to places unknown. But with their tight bond to this location, one can only wonder if the spirits of the past will continue to be attached to the property forever, dancing the night way at their beloved Sooner Corral.

CHAPTER 9

I'll Take Mine Medium Rare, With a Side of Ghost

For a fun night out, you might join your family for a movie and a meal at your favorite restaurant. But what if that restaurant served up something other than just a delicious meal? There are several haunted eateries across the United States, but in Oklahoma City there is one that stands above the rest. It's known as the Cattleman's Steakhouse.

Located in the heart of the stockyards, Cattleman's was established in 1910, making it one of the oldest restaurants in Oklahoma. No wonder the place is haunted. Known for its delicious steaks, the restaurant has played host to many famous people and celebrities. John Wayne, US President Ronald Regan, country singer Reba McIntire, and the movie star Sylvester Stallone, have all stopped in for one of the country's best steaks. Its reputation began to build in the early years when Oklahoma

had just become a state. The Stockyard, or Packingtown as it was once called, served as a main center for the thousands of herds of cattle being driven from Texas to Kansas. I don't know about you, but I personally enjoy a good steak. However, I'm not sure I could enjoy one while seeing a herd of cows being driven down the road right outside of the place where I was going to eat one. After all, have you ever seen a cow up close? They remind me of an oversized puppy dog with those big brown eyes. Considering how many steaks have been served up over the years at this place it's a wonder that the place isn't haunted by a bunch of cows.

There have been many owners of Cattleman's over the years, but one stands out among them all. He didn't purchase the business like most people would. Instead, he won it in a very luck roll of the dice. His name was Gene Wade. Some might say he was at the right place at the right time. He was taking his turn at throwing the dice when a man next to him asked if he would care to make a wager. He told Gene that if he could toss a hard six (both dice landing on a 3), he could take over ownership of his restaurant. With a blow on the dice and a shake of the hand, Gene tossed the two cubes in the air. All eyes were on the dice as they tumbled down the table. A collective gasp could be heard among the deafening silence of the room as the dice toppled to a stop. To everyone's disbelief, the two small dice found their final resting place, revealing three small dots on top of each cube. Gene Wade had just won the rights to Cattleman's steak house. His luck forever remembered as he branded the numbers three and three along the walls of his newly found fortune and can still be seen today marking the walls of the Cattleman's restaurant.

Can you imagine what your life would be like if you won such a prize? His life was changed overnight. Perhaps that might be reason enough to continue to stay here even after death. There are rumored to be several spirits still roaming the rooms of the restaurant. Could Gene be one of them? People often report hearing disembodied footsteps (that's where you can hear someone walking but no one is around to see). Some have felt cold spots in the building even on the hottest days of summer. Others have felt the touch of an unseen hand. Then, of course, there is the old rocking chair. Located toward the front of the building near the door, a rocking chair sits empty, positioned in the direction of the dining area. It is said that it belonged to one of the past owners who would often sit in the chair looking out at his patrons, rocking softly and bidding them a hello or goodbye. Rumor has it that from time to time his spirit comes back and takes a seat in his favorite chair slowly rocking, as he watches over the place.

Some of the other spirits that inhabit the place are believed to be customers

or employees from the Prohibition era. Cattleman's was considered a family restaurant or cattleman's café, but it also had its dark side once. Prohibition was a trying time for most people. Money was scarce. Alcohol was banned, but those who traded it illegally could make a quick buck. Many businesses had secret back-room businesses known as "speakeasies" during that time. Alcohol, dancing girls, illegal distilleries, and gambling could be found in these speakeasies if you knew who to ask. It was a lawless and dangerous business to be in

and often people would end up seriously hurt or worse: dead.

Perhaps some of the spirits that still reside here could be lingering from the time of wild parties and bootlegging, hoping the party would never end. Whatever the reason, the spirits in Cattleman's continue to hang on with each passing year. And the steaks remain a cut above the rest in Oklahoma City's Stockyard district.

CHAPTER 10

Lights, Camera, Action

It's a Saturday night in your small hometown. The latest movie is playing at your local theater. You grabbed your five-cent popcorn and a bottle of soda and you find your seat among the crowd. You and a group of your friends wait anxiously for the music to play. A woman in her Sunday best sits poised at the piano ready to start the show. The curtains open and her fingers start to drum quickly along the keys. The show has finally begun. You sit in wonder as the magic of movies begin to play out. Words jump across the screen as the black and white images of overly dramatic actors flit across the screen. You dodge a locomotive as it races toward you, convinced the image will hurl itself at you. It's the early days of cinema in Oklahoma City. It's the dawn of a new era, one of wonder, magic, and imagination as the movie industry changes lives, bringing entertainment to anyone who steps foot into the world of the moving picture shows.

The creation of the movie industry started around the same time as the statehood of Oklahoma. Like many people across the US, the residents of Oklahoma longed for entertainment. The new movie industry was happy to oblige. Unfortunately, Hollywood was a world away and getting movies to a theater across the country wasn't an easy task back then.

Today we stream movies directly to our phones. It was a much more complicated process one hundred years ago. Movies came on long strips of film, which contained highly flammable chemicals. The were stored in round tin containers. One small mishap could ruin an entire film or worse, cause a deadly fire. Oklahoma City was in the heart of the state, the perfect location for distributing films to theaters in surrounding towns. Soon, part of the film industry started to grow in the downtown area better known as the Oklahoma Film

Exchange. Theater owners could come from around the state and, for a small fee, view the latest movies and decide which ones to show in their own theaters. With the advancement of technology, the need for the film exchange began to die off, leaving what was known as Film Row abandoned. The buildings here sat vacant year after year and Film Row became an abandoned and dangerous part of town.

Many years later, stories started to emerge about the ghostly presence of those who chose to stay behind here. Stories began to circulate about the old Paramount building. There are several spirits rumored to haunt it. One of the most well-known spirits is that of a man who resides in the projector room of the building's movie theater. Many people have reported seeing a ghostly man's face peering down at them from the small window of the projection room. But when they head to the room to confront him, no one is anywhere to be seen. The door to the room is often found unlocked or open just minutes after it had been locked.

Another spirit grabbing attention here is that of a woman who hangs around in the basement. Perhaps you don't believe in ghosts? Well, neither did the gentleman in our next story. But it seems the spirit had other things in mind. While playing a game of darts in the basement, the man heard a female voice say, "Well, hello." Turning to see who had joined him, he was taken aback as he realized he was the only one there. The only living person, that is. He brushed the incident off and carried on about his business. Then he heard the voice once again. He turned quickly, hoping to catch the intruder. But he was once again met with the emptiness of the room. He left the room as quickly as he could, refusing to go back there alone again.

There are other stories connected to the Paramount building: disembodied voices, shadowy figures, cold sorts, doors opening and closing on their own. The building itself holds mysteries and secrets. There have been many renovations through the years and now there are hidden hallways and even a staircase that

leads to nowhere. The secrets of these places may never be known. Once, while removing some old boards, construction workers found a splatter pattern of a dark red substance on the wall. The police were notified, and the substance was tested. It was human blood. But with no body or other evidence of a crime, the splattered blood remained a mystery. Perhaps it belonged to one of the resident spirits who

continues to walk these darkened halls waiting patiently for its death to be resolved. Whatever their reason, these spirits continue to live on in the Paramount picture film exchange.

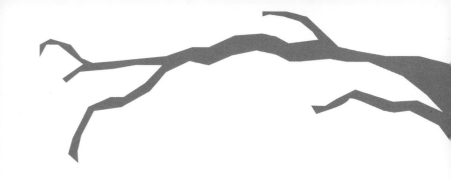

Conclusion

Through the years, many things have changed in and around Oklahoma City. Families have come and gone. Buildings have risen and fallen. Technology has made its mark on this land. Teepees and sod houses have been replaced with skyscrapers and casinos. Horses, buggies, and trains have been replaced with cars and planes. The one-room schoolhouses which once contained all grade levels of children have now grown to a college campus size with thousands of young students roaming its halls.

Economic growth and time have brought about a new world, forever changing the nation's last frontier. Despite these changes, some things will never change. The spirits of the people who fought to develop this land as well as the spirits of those who lived here long before will mark this territory forever. As you walk along the streets of Oklahoma City or visit some of its historic sites, try to imagine

what life was like so many years ago. Feel the energy that surrounds you. Strain your ears to hear the voices of its past. If you're lucky, you might just get a glimpse of one of the residents from long ago as you revisit the ghosts of Oklahoma City.

Tanya McCoy is the founder of the Oklahoma Paranormal Association and has actively investigated haunted locations for over a decade. Prior to that she spent over twenty years researching various parts of the paranormal field. She currently teaches classes on paranormal research, paranormal research vs. quantum physics, cryptids, psychic development and research, and myths and folklore.

Check out some of the other Spooky America titles available now!

Spooky America was adapted from the creeptastic Haunted America series for adults. Haunted America explores historical haunts in cities and regions across America. Each book chronicles both the widely known and less-familiar history behind local ghosts and other unexplained mysteries. Here's more from *Haunted Oklahoma City* author Tanya McCoy:

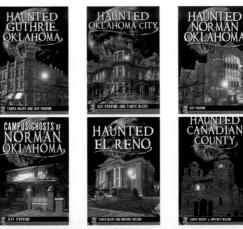